THE SECRET WORLD OF

Butterflies and Moths

THE SECRET WORLD OF
Butterflies and Moths

Ken Preston-Mafham

www.raintreepublishers.co.uk
Visit our website to find out more information about **Raintree** books.

To order:
 Phone 44 (0) 1865 888112
 Send a fax to 44 (0) 1865 314091
 Visit the Raintree Bookshop at www.raintreepublishers.co.uk to browse our catalogue and
order online.

First published in Great Britain by Raintree,
Halley Court, Jordan Hill, Oxford
OX2 8EJ, part of Harcourt Education.
Raintree is a registered trademark of Harcourt Education Ltd.

Produced for Raintree by Discovery Books
Editors: Sarah Jameson, Kathryn Walker and
Catherine Clarke
Series Consultant: Michael Chinery
Design: Ian Winton
Illustrations: Stuart Lafford
Production: Jonathan Smith

Originated by Dot Gradations Ltd
Printed and bound in China by South China Printing
Company

ISBN 1 844 21585 7
07 06 05 04 03
10 9 8 7 6 5 4 3 2 1

British Library Cataloguing in Publication Data
Preston-Mafham, Ken
The Secret World of Butterflies and Moths
595.7'8
A full catalogue record for this book is available from the
British Library.

Acknowledgements
The publishers would like to thank the following for
permission to reproduce photographs:
Bruce Coleman Collection p. 13 (Kim Taylor), 23 (Jorg &
Petra Wegner), 26 (Kim Taylor), 29 (Jane Burton), 31 top
(Hans Reinhard), 37 top (Natural Selection Inc.), 42
(Pacific Stock), 43 (David Middleton); London Scientific
Films/Oxford Scientific Films p. 8; Natural History
Photographic Agency pp. 11 (A. P. Barnes), 14 (Daniel
Zupanc) 15 (Stephen Dalton), 17 top, 19 and 20 (Stephen
Dalton), 21 (Anthony Bannister), 22 (Dr Ivan Polunin),
24 and 33 (Anthony Bannister), 34/35 (Stephen Dalton),
35 top (Jany Sauvanet), 41 top (A.N.T.); Oxford Scientific
Films pp. 16/17 (Doug Wechsler), 38 (Peter Gould),
40/41 (Chris R. Sharp); Premaphotos Wildlife pp. 9, 10,
28, 30, 31 bottom, 36, 37 bottom and 39 (Ken Preston-
Mafham), 32 (Jean Preston-Mafham).
All background images © Steck-Vaughn Collection
(Corbis Royalty Free, Getty Royalty Free, and
StockBYTE).

Cover photograph reproduced with permission of the
Natural History Photographic Agency (A.P. Barnes).

Every effort has been made to contact copyright holders of
any material reproduced in this book. Any omissions will
be rectified in subsequent printings if notice is given to
the publishers.

Any words appearing in the text in bold, **like this**, are explained in the Glossary.

Contents

What are butterflies and moths? 6

Butterfly or moth? 12

Where are they found? 16

Courtship and mating 20

Life cycles 24

Food and feeding 30

Enemies and survival 34

Hibernation and migration 40

Butterflies, moths and people 42

Glossary 44

Further information 46

Index 47

What are butterflies and moths?

 The smallest butterfly is the pygmy blue from the USA, with a wingspan of only 13–19 millimetres.

 The largest butterfly to be found in Britain is the monarch, with a wingspan of 109 millimetres – but only 200 have been seen there since the first in 1876. The biggest butterfly of all is Queen Alexandra's birdwing, from the island of New Guinea in the Pacific Ocean, which can measure over 280 millimetres from wing tip to wing tip.

 With a wingspan of nearly 300 millimetres, the world's biggest moth is the Agrippa moth from South America.

 Many tiny moths have wingspans of only 3 millimetres.

Butterflies and moths are closely related kinds of insects that can be difficult to tell apart. Although small, they are some of the most remarkable and beautiful creatures on Earth, undergoing a magical **metamorphosis**, or change, from wriggling larvae, usually called caterpillars, to beautiful and delicate-winged adults. They belong to a large group called the Lepidoptera, which comes from two Greek words meaning 'scale' and 'wing'. This is because of the thousands of tiny scales that form a closely fitting coat on the very colourful wings of most butterflies and many moths.

There are about 15,000 **species** of butterflies in the world and more than 150,000 species of moths. Someone who collects or studies these insects is called a lepidopterist.

THE ADULT BODY

Like all insects, butterflies and moths have six legs. The skeleton of an insect is on the outside of the body, and is called an exoskeleton. Humans have 'endoskeletons' – on the inside. Insect skeletons contain all the soft organs within the outer casing. In humans, the soft organs 'hang' on to the framework of the inner skeleton. Butterflies and moths have soft exoskeletons compared with insects such as beetles, and they can be easily damaged if carelessly handled.

Curiously, some moths have 'ears' on their bodies that detect the echolocation sounds given off by bats hunting for a tasty meal. When it hears the approaching bat, the moth can dive for cover and escape being caught.

Butterflies spend a lot of time sipping nectar from flowers. The striking American tiger swallowtail butterfly feeds on thistle heads, a favourite flower of many butterflies.

wings
There are four wings (two forewings and two hindwings) that work together in flight.

forewing

hindwing

compound eye
Large eye made up of many, tiny hexagonal lenses.

antennae
Small sense organs for smelling are scattered over the surface of the antennae.

proboscis
Long, flexible tongue for sucking up nectar and other liquid food.

abdomen
Segmented tail area that contains the heart, reproductive organs and most of the digestive system.

thorax
Middle part of the body, between the head and abdomen.

THE HEAD

A butterfly or moth's head is small and slightly rounded. This is where the parts used for feeding, the eyes and the **antennae** can be found. The eyes are not like ours. They are made up of thousands of tiny individual lenses that fit neatly together like a complicated pattern. These **compound eyes** can sense movement very well, which is why it can be so difficult to sneak up on a resting butterfly.

This is a large white butterfly, commonly found in gardens. You can see the proboscis, coiled tightly, and the large compound eye made up of many tiny lenses.

However, compound eyes cannot see detail as well as we can.

Moths and butterflies do not have noses. It is their antennae that pick up smells and, in butterflies, also help them to balance. The antennae of some male moths are so sensitive that they can smell the scent of a female many kilometres away.

FLEXIBLE TONGUES

Most adult butterflies and moths do not have jaws and therefore cannot bite or chew their food. Instead, they have a long, flexible feeding tube called a proboscis. This is hollow, like a drinking straw, and is used to suck up liquid food. When not being used, the proboscis is coiled neatly out of the way beneath the head, but it can be unrolled quickly when needed. The proboscis of a sphinx moth from Madagascar is around 300 millimetres long – several times longer than the moth's own body. This allows it to reach the sweet nectar in the long **style** of certain orchids. Some adult moths do not have a proboscis at all, but instead have jaws and chew their food (mainly pollen from flowers).

Like other sphinx moths (also called hawkmoths), this hummingbird hawkmoth can hover in front of a flower while its proboscis reaches inside for nectar.

WINGS

Butterflies and moths have two pairs of wings (forewings and hindwings) usually covered in thousands of tiny scales overlapping one another, like the tiles on a roof. These scales are easily brushed off, which is why it is important not to handle butterflies and moths by their wings.

Some butterflies, like the glasswing and clearwing, have wings that are almost transparent. Some moths, like the females of the bagworm and winter moth, have no wings at all.

The wings are made stronger by a network of tiny branching tubes called veins. These help to support the wing as it moves and carries the insect during flight. Flight speeds can reach up to 54 kilometres per hour (34 miles per hour) in some types of hawkmoth, while the monarch butterfly has been known to reach speeds of 37 kilometres per hour (23 miles per hour).

The wings of this African butterfly have hardly any scales, making them almost transparent. Transparent-winged butterflies are found mainly in the rainforest, where they fly around in the deep gloom beneath the trees.

Preparing to fly

In cold weather, the wing muscles of butterflies and moths must be 'warmed up' in order to work properly. Butterflies, like this swallowtail, absorb **solar energy** by lying in the sunshine with their wings outstretched. Moths, however, are **nocturnal** (active at night), so they warm up their flying muscles by vibrating their wings very fast for a few minutes before taking off.

BUTTERFLIES AND MOTHS WITH TAILS

Several kinds of butterflies and moths have tails sticking out from the rear edge of their hindwings. Swallowtail butterflies are the best known for this feature, although not all of them have tails. Swallowtail moths are found in **tropical** countries and have bright metallic colours. Some moon moths have very long tails, much longer than any butterfly.

Butterfly or moth?

It is not always easy to tell the difference between a butterfly and a moth. One way is to look at the wings. Usually, a moth will rest with wings folded flat over its body like a little tent, while a butterfly will hold its wings pressed tightly together and pointing upwards, over its back.

The spurge hawkmoth has feathery antennae and a plump, furry body. Its wings lie flat out to either side.

Butterflies are usually brightly coloured and tend to fly during the day.

Sometimes it is only the male butterfly that is an eye-catching colour. Bright blue males and brown females are quite a common pairing.

Moths are mostly active at night, and their colours are usually dull. Bright colours would draw attention to a moth resting by day and would be invisible in the darkness when it becomes active.

There are exceptions to the general colour rule, such as brown or earth-coloured butterflies and moths that are multicoloured and active only in bright sunlight.

Butterflies, like the brimstone, often hold their wings high over their backs, which moths never do. The thin, club-ended antennae and slim abdomen are both typical of butterflies.

However, many butterflies and moths hold their wings out flat at their sides. Fortunately, there are other **identifying** features, such as the **antennae**, or long 'feelers', on top of the head. A butterfly's antennae look like very thin pencils, with thickened, club-like tips, whereas those of a moth usually look like hairs or tiny feathers. Moths also tend to have much larger, fatter bodies in relation to their wings and to be more furry than butterflies.

Wing scales

It is the wing scales that are responsible for the brilliant colours of many butterflies and moths. These colours are produced in two different ways. Either the colour is contained in the scales like paint (red and yellow are two of the colours produced like this) or the scales are not actually coloured at all but have a special shape that breaks up and reflects light. This results in the bright, flashing metallic blue often seen on butterflies. Below you can see the wing scales of a swallowtail butterfly close-up.

I DIDN'T KNOW THAT

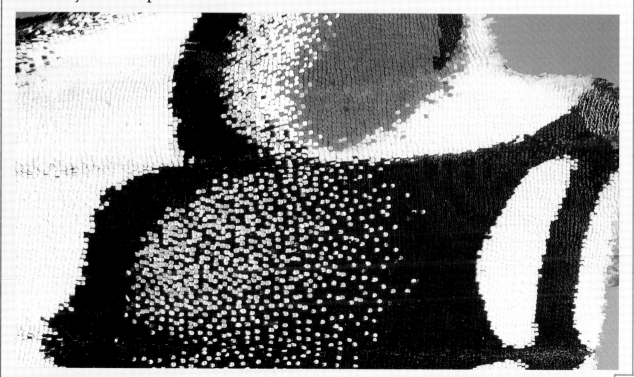

SKIPPERS – BUTTERFLIES OR MOTHS?

Skippers get their name from the darting, bobbing and lively patterns of their flight.

The long-tailed skipper is from North America. Like other skippers, it flies along quickly, close to the ground.

A heath fritillary butterfly feeds. The undersides of a fritillary's wings are beautifully marked with silver spots.

They have always been included in the butterfly family, but in certain ways skippers are more like moths.

They have quite fat, hairy bodies and some rest with their wings flat, rather than held up above their back. In fact, skippers share features of both moths and butterflies.

BUTTERFLY AND MOTH FAMILIES

Butterflies are usually divided into four families (five, if you include the skippers). Often, it can be easy to tell which family a butterfly belongs to. Most large butterflies with tails are swallowtails. Butterflies that are mainly white or yellow in colour belong to the family of whites and sulphurs. Many of their caterpillars feed on plants from the cabbage and mustard family.

This elephant hawkmoth shows how the front and back pairs of wings beat together. With their fast blur of wings, hawkmoths are quick and powerful in flight.

Brush-footed butterflies are easy to spot because they walk on only four of their six legs. The front two are too small to use for walking. This large family includes the fritillaries and browns, as well as the famous monarchs and the mourning cloaks. Coppers and blues are small butterflies, often with bright metallic colours, and belong to a family that also includes the hairstreaks.

There are so many moth families that telling them apart is not easy, especially as many moths are extremely small. The emperor moth family includes some of the largest and most interesting

species of all. Many of these species have large eye spots on their wings. Sphinx or hawkmoths are fat, heavy-bodied moths with a powerful, fast zooming style of flight. They often hover in front of flowers as they feed, and some can fly backwards as easily as forwards. At the other end of the size scale, bell moths are quite small, and their caterpillars are often pests. The apple-codling moth caterpillar, for example, can be a nasty surprise if you bite into an apple it has invaded. The small caterpillar of the clothes moth can nibble holes in your clothes, before eventually turning into a harmless adult.

Where are they found?

Butterflies and moths are found in most parts of the world. They live in many different kinds of places, from the bedroom of an urban house to gardens, parks, forests, deserts, grasslands and mountains. The only places you won't find them are the very driest deserts and areas where there is always ice and snow. For example, the highest mountain tops and polar ice caps.

Along the banks of this South American rainforest stream, you would probably find one or two shade-loving clearwing butterflies. At the edge of a wider river, however, where there is more light, masses of butterflies may be found feeding on riverside flowers, or on salty sand by the water's edge.

In some tropical rainforests, more than 100 types of butterfly can easily be seen in a single day.

After heavy rain in the normally dry Atacama Desert of Chile, adult butterflies and moths may suddenly appear after being away for ten years or longer.

Some butterflies can only live in certain places. For example, the Sand Creek variety of the American Great Basin fritillary butterfly is only found in volcanic areas in the state of Oregon, USA.

In North America, many butterflies and moths that live on the prairies are helped by regular grass fires, which keep their habitat from becoming overgrown with trees.

RAINFORESTS

The richest **habitats** are the **tropical** rainforests, especially those of the Amazon region of South America.

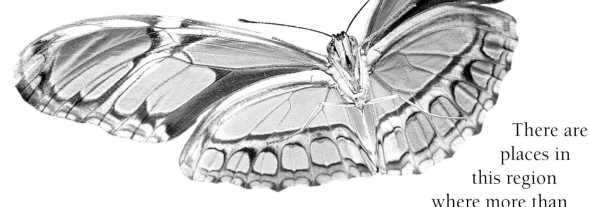

▲ The rainforests are home to many spectacular butterflies. The beautiful, green malachite longwing butterfly comes from South America.

There are places in this region where more than 1500 different kinds of butterflies may be found in an area the size of Hyde Park in London. This is more than are found in the whole of Europe, North America and Australia added together! Rainforest butterflies, especially the larger kinds like swallowtails, tend to spend most of their time high up in the tops of the trees and are rarely seen near ground level. A few kinds, such as glasswings and others with transparent wings, live on the gloomy forest floor, flitting silently around in the permanent shadows. As night falls in these forests, many hundreds of **species** of moths may also be seen by setting up a **light trap** to attract them.

DESERTS

Deserts are a particularly difficult environment for butterflies and moths, although many of them have **adapted** for life in these dry lands. In the deserts of south-western USA, the caterpillars of giant **skippers** live inside agave and yucca stems. These are tough, thick-leaved plants that grow all the year round, even in dry seasons. Some moth caterpillars burrow inside moist, juicy cactus stems, which are also found growing all year.

In some desert **species** the caterpillars grow very rapidly during the short time after seasonal rains, when there are lots of wildflowers to eat. The **pupae** (see page 28) can survive in a **dormant** state for many years, until rains trigger the emergence of the butterflies.

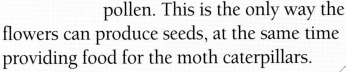

I DIDN'T KNOW THAT

A desert relationship

Yucca moth caterpillars live inside yucca plant flowers in the deserts of North America. The caterpillars feed on the seeds of the plant and the female moth makes sure there are enough seeds to eat. Before laying her eggs in a yucca flower, she pierces a hole in its base and stuffs it full of pollen. This is the only way the flowers can produce seeds, at the same time providing food for the moth caterpillars.

TEMPERATE FORESTS AND GRASSLANDS

In Europe, North America and eastern Asia, where the year is broken by long, cold winters, there are not as many butterflies and moths as there are in the **tropical** rainforests.

Temperate forests and grasslands are often not permanent **habitats**, but change over the years. The level of change can depend on various events, such as grass fires, the amount of animal grazing and interference by humans. If the grazing of

Summer meadows in temperate areas such as Europe and North America are often full of wildflowers, which attract butterflies. This painted lady belongs to the world's most widely spread family of butterflies.

grasslands by animals like cattle or sheep stops – scrub, bushes and eventually woodland will take over and the grassland butterflies and moths will die out.

As a rule, blues and skippers are typical grassland or open country butterflies, while hairstreaks and many fritillaries are often found in woodland habitats.

Courtship and mating

Moths, which usually fly at night, find each other using a special scent. Butterflies, which fly during the day, mainly use sight.

For some butterflies, female scent is very important. Even a female pupa will attract a crowd of possible butterfly mates.

Male monarch butterflies chase the females and catch them in flight, taking them to the ground, where mating takes place.

After they have mated once, some female butterflies are unable to mate again.

Individual members of a specific butterfly and moth **species** are often widely scattered, making it difficult for the males and females to find one another in order to mate.

In some butterfly families, the male stakes out a **territory** to which the female will come for mating. The territory could be a desert hilltop, as in the case of the black swallowtail and great purple hairstreak, or a sunlit spot in the forest as preferred by the speckled wood. These butterflies chase away other males, so that when a female finally arrives to mate, she is likely to choose him rather than any

Male green longhorn moths form dancing swarms, which attract females looking for a mate. These males are just beginning to take off, having landed on some flowers for a rest.

competitor. Sometimes the females are able to take their pick from a swarm of males, as in many of the tiny, day-flying longhorned moths. The males form 'dancing groups' in the air around a tree branch, and the females join them just long enough to choose a mate.

Other male butterflies actively look for females by 'patrolling' along an area where females are likely to be resting. These patrollers tend to be members of very common species, or those that live in crowded conditions in a restricted environment. Patrolling greatly increases the chances of a male finding a female.

Amazing antennae

Many male moths, like this African moon moth, have very exaggerated comb-like **antennae**. These are designed to act as 'scent-aerials' and can pick up tiny amounts of a special scent given off by a faraway female. She may be as far as 11 kilometres (6½ miles) away, but the male's antennae accurately guide him towards her, following the extremely faint traces of her scent wafting on the breeze.

I DIDN'T KNOW THAT

COURTSHIP

Female insects will not necessarily mate with any male who comes along. In fact, a male may not even be recognized as a possible partner, unless he first takes steps to show his sex and identity. This means that a period of 'courtship' will often be needed before the female decides to accept her mate.

In butterfly courtship, the male usually flutters over and around the female. He brushes against her, bombarding her with scent from special scales on his wings called **androconia**. They are easily broken off during the male's energetic courtship flutterings and act as tiny 'love-bombs', encouraging the female to want to mate. In some butterflies the male's scent comes from brush-like structures called hair pencils that can stick out from the tip of the lower body. Some male butterflies give the female a 'hug', holding her scent-sensitive **antennae** between their wings. This makes sure that the antennae are really drenched in the male's scent.

Many male moths also shower the female with scent during courtship. The scent comes from scent-brushes on the leg.

Moths mate in a back-to-back position, and may spend many hours sitting still on a leaf. This beautiful species is from the rainforests of south-east Asia. Its brilliant colours warn enemies that it tastes nasty.

MATING

Mating takes place in a back-to-back position, with the male and female facing in opposite directions. Although it looks awkward, they are still able to fly like this. In many **species** the male does all the flying and carries the female, dangling beneath him. Mating is usually quite a long process and may take several hours, sometimes lasting overnight. If a female does not want to mate, she holds the tip of her body upward, out of the male's reach.

Like moths, butterflies also mate facing in opposite directions. These brush-footed butterflies from the South American rainforests stand on only four of their six legs.

23

Life cycles

- **During the lifetime of a large female moth, she may lay up to 20,000 eggs.**

- **Many butterfly caterpillars, such as the large white, spin a silken belt, like a little silk rope, around their middle to support the pupa.**

- **The cocoon of the flannel moth has a trapdoor that snaps open when the adult pushes against it.**

- **Arctic caterpillars may take two years to grow fully, because of the very short summers and low temperatures.**

- **Most adult butterflies and moths probably live for only two to three weeks.**

Like other insects, such as beetles, wasps and flies, butterflies and moths develop through four very different life stages: egg, larva, **pupa** and adult.

THE EGG

Female butterflies and moths usually take great care in placing their eggs where their caterpillars will best be able to grow – normally on a **foodplant**. It is common to see a female butterfly flitting from plant to plant, landing for a moment before moving on. She is making a quick test of a variety of leaves, to

This female emperor moth from South Africa is laying eggs on a plant stem. At first the eggs are almost white, but as they age and the caterpillars begin to develop inside, they gradually darken in colour.

Ant protection

Some female butterflies only lay their eggs close to ants that will help protect the caterpillar from enemies. The caterpillars give off **nutrient**-rich droplets that the ants like to eat. In this way, the ants and caterpillars are helping each other – this is called symbiosis.

find out which one is suitable as food for her caterpillars. She quickly 'tastes' each leaf using special chemical feelers on her feet, her **antennae** or on the tip of her body.

Most **species** lay their eggs on the actual foodplant, but others simply drop their eggs here and there as they fly over the grasses on which their caterpillars will later feed. The eggs may be placed alone or in batches. The number of eggs in a batch can vary from 10 to about 350 for butterflies, depending upon the species. The eggs themselves are usually shiny, most often white, pale yellow, or green. They are often beautifully shaped, like little coloured parcels, with detailed surface patterns and ribs down the

sides. Some moths, such as most tussock moths, protect their eggs underneath masses of hairs removed from their bodies. In others, such as the American tent-caterpillar moth, the egg-batch forms a wide ring around a twig of the foodplant.

Once laid, most eggs are left, but in at least two kinds of **tropical** butterflies the female stays and guards them. Most eggs hatch within a week or less. Some moths and butterflies, like the white admiral, have only one set of offspring (or brood) per year. Others, such as the copper, have two or more, and in areas where it is always warm some species mate all year.

THE LARVAL STAGES

The larvae of butterflies and moths are usually called caterpillars. They may be smooth, hairy or spiny. After hatching from the eggs, the first thing that many caterpillars do is to eat their eggshells, which are extremely **nutritious**. Caterpillars do not look like the adults; they are really just long, wiggly eating-machines. Their main aim in life is to eat as much food as possible.

When the caterpillar hatches, its first meal is usually the eggshell. This is full of nutrients, which are too good to waste. This owl butterfly caterpillar from South America will eventually reach a length of more than 10 centimetres.

THE CATERPILLAR BODY

Although some caterpillars appear smooth-skinned, they are in fact covered with many fine bristles or hairs.

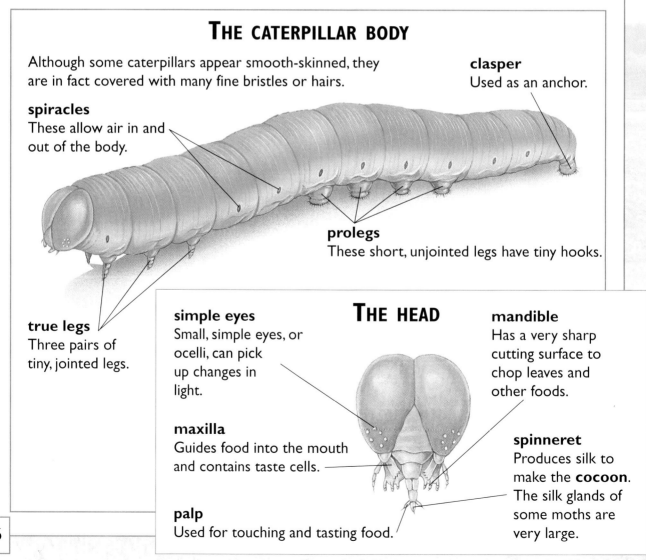

clasper
Used as an anchor.

spiracles
These allow air in and out of the body.

prolegs
These short, unjointed legs have tiny hooks.

true legs
Three pairs of tiny, jointed legs.

THE HEAD

simple eyes
Small, simple eyes, or ocelli, can pick up changes in light.

maxilla
Guides food into the mouth and contains taste cells.

palp
Used for touching and tasting food.

mandible
Has a very sharp cutting surface to chop leaves and other foods.

spinneret
Produces silk to make the **cocoon**. The silk glands of some moths are very large.

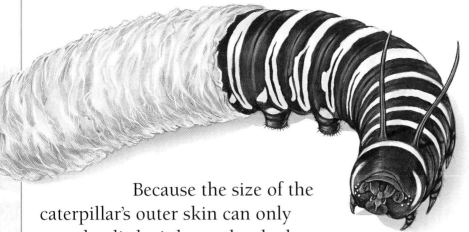

Because the size of the caterpillar's outer skin can only stretch a little, it has to be shed, or moulted, each time the caterpillar wants to grow larger. Growth therefore happens in stages. The caterpillar quickly expands into its soft new skin, shortly after moulting out of the tough old one. Most caterpillars moult five times as they grow up.

Unlike most adult butterflies and moths, caterpillars have powerful jaws and can crunch and tear their food. The head is tough and rounded and does not have the **compound eyes** of the adult. Instead, there is a group of about six tiny, simple eyes called **ocelli**. These eyes cannot see a picture of the world around them, but can tell light from dark. The head also has a pair of very short **antennae** that can hardly be seen, unlike the long antennae of the adult.

Like the adults, caterpillars have three pairs of jointed legs at the front end of the body. In addition, caterpillars have several pairs of quite fleshy and stumpy legs towards the back of the body. These are called prolegs. Equipped with tiny hooks, they are very good at hanging tightly on to things.

When colourful cinnabar moth caterpillars feed on leaves, their claspers and prolegs cling tightly to the stem.

The time taken for the caterpillar to grow fully is usually three to six weeks, depending on the **species** and the temperature of its surroundings.

27

THE PUPAL STAGE

The caterpillar eventually stops feeding and starts to wander around, looking for a good place in which to make one last moult into a **pupa**. In butterflies this pupa is called a chrysalis, meaning 'golden', and it may be beautifully spotted with silver or gold flecks. In moths, the pupa is most often a dark, shiny reddish-brown. Pupae may form in the soil, under a stone or in a curled leaf of the **foodplant**, or out in the open on a plant, tree or rock. Many butterfly pupae hang upside down from a silken pad fixed to a plant or rock.

The caterpillar of this South African moth has decorated the silk of its cocoon with a protective coat of stinging hairs from its own back. To make the cocoon more difficult to see, it has also included a few pieces of leaf, which have died and turned brown.

PUPATION

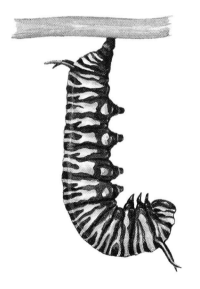

1. A monarch caterpillar attaches itself to a twig with its claspers and hangs down ready to pupate.

2. Its skin splits and rolls back to reveal the soft pupa underneath.

3. Inside the hardened pupa case, the caterpillar changes into a butterfly. Tiny holes in the case allow air in and out.

Hanging on the empty husk of its chrysalis, this newly hatched adult comma butterfly still has to pump up its wings. They are crumpled after being tightly folded inside the chrysalis.

Some moth pupae are protected underneath a mass of hairs. Many pupae, especially those of moths, surround themselves with a thick jacket of silk. This is called a **cocoon** and is spun by the caterpillar before turning into a pupa. All caterpillars can produce this silk from special glands in their mouths. Many **species** spend the winter in the pupal stage, so the adult does not appear until the following spring. During this time, it cannot eat or drink because its mouthparts are sealed over.

It is inside the pupa that the amazing **metamorphosis** from worm-like, wingless caterpillar to fully-winged adult takes place. Inside the tough pupa, the larval structures are broken down and replaced by those of the adult. After an average of ten to fourteen days, the adult butterfly or moth breaks free of the pupa. It then pumps blood into its soft, crumpled wings to expand them to full size. After about 15 to 30 minutes, it can take to the air and fly away.

Food and feeding

Some moths from the American tropics live in the fur of tree sloths; the females lay their eggs on the sloth's dung, on which the caterpillars then feed.

Some moth caterpillars live in spider webs, eating the remains of creatures caught in the web.

The death's-head hawkmoth enters honeybee hives to steal the honey.

Dung left by animals such as lions and leopards can attract a mass of feeding butterflies.

▶ This red-headed monster is the large and brightly coloured caterpillar of the frangipani hawkmoth of South America. Its powerful jaws can easily munch through leaves and stalks as it holds on tightly with hook-like true legs.

CATERPILLAR FOOD

The only goal in a caterpillar's life is to feed and survive. Unlike the adult, it does not have to find a mate or lay eggs. To achieve this goal, caterpillars pack away as much food as possible during each feeding session.

Most caterpillars feed on leaves, using their tough jaws to bite bits off and chew them up. Because leaves are not highly **nutritious**, large quantities are needed if the caterpillar is to grow rapidly. Some caterpillars eat only flowers or buds, while others eat fungi. Other caterpillars, such as those of the carpenterworm and leopard moth, tunnel into the woody stems of trees and bushes. They often take three to four years to develop fully, because wood is a very poor quality of food to live on.

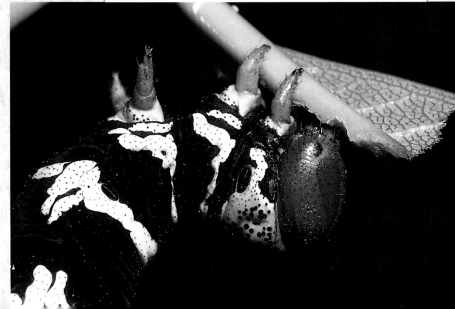

When feeding in large numbers, caterpillars can reduce their **foodplant** to shreds. This cabbage is being turned into a skeleton by the many hungry mouths of large white butterfly caterpillars, which always feed in groups.

As well as feeding on plants, caterpillars eat a wide variety of other things. The caterpillars of some blue butterflies eat ant larvae, while others eat aphids or planthopper bugs. The stick-like caterpillars of two kinds of Hawaiian moths catch and eat flies. Many tiny moth caterpillars have strange diets and eat the waxy cells inside honeybee nests, or wool, fur, clothes, carpets and feathers. Some caterpillars, like those of the California tent moth, feed in such huge numbers on certain trees that they strip them bare of all their leaves.

Leaf mining

The caterpillars of many small moths actually live inside the leaves on which they feed. They eat away the green tissues in the narrow space between the upper and lower surfaces of the leaf. Their feeding activities create a 'leaf mine', which can be seen as a pale blotch or squiggly line on the leaf.

I DIDN'T KNOW THAT

ADULT FOOD

Adult butterflies and moths do not usually spend as much time on feeding as their offspring. In fact, some kinds do not feed at all in the adult stage. As few adults have jaws, most of them can take food only in liquid form. They sip rather than chew their food. Many butterflies and moths feed on the nectar from flowers, probing into them with their proboscis. Nectar is rich in sugars and provides much of the energy needed for flight.

Some small moths have chewing mouthparts and therefore can eat the pollen on flowers. Ripe fruits are also attractive to many adult moths and butterflies, especially when they are damaged and leaking an attractive sweet juice. The sap leaking from damaged tree bark, or the liquid from animal remains, are also attractive and tasty to many butterflies and moths.

Flower nectar is the favourite food of many adult butterflies. The black proboscis of this monarch is clearly seen as it probes into a zinnia flower to suck up the sugar-rich nectar.

The males of many butterflies and some moths spend long periods of time drinking from the damp, salty ground, because they need the **sodium** to be able to mate. If the ground is dry, they will sometimes squirt liquid out of their proboscis to moisten it. They may also land on the skin of a human to feed on their sweat, which also contains sodium. They can be very hard to get rid of. Some moths go one step further and regularly feed on the tears coming from the eyes of animals such as elephants, buffalo,

In many parts of the world, but especially in the **tropical** regions, it is common to see large groups of male butterflies feeding on salty ground or on animal dung. These striking butterflies are from Africa.

cattle and deer. Harvester butterflies tap into the liquid contained in woolly aphids (soft-bodied insects), but the prize for the most gruesome diet goes to the Asian vampire moth, which pierces the skin of mammals (including humans) with its sharply pointed proboscis to suck their blood.

33

Enemies and survival

Like most insects, 98 per cent of butterflies and moths do not reach adulthood. **Predators**, **parasites**, and diseases, as well as human activities, kill a high percentage of them at every stage in the life cycle. Enemies of moths and butterflies include birds, monkeys, bats, lizards, frogs, praying mantises, assassin bugs, stink bugs, robber flies, hunting wasps and spiders.

Because of their loose-fitting covering of wing scales, butterflies can be difficult to catch. This chameleon has made a direct hit on a butterfly with its sticky tongue, but has only succeeded in knocking off a few scales, sending the butterfly tumbling off its flower.

The larvae of certain parasitic flies and wasps develop inside the living bodies of many caterpillars. After eating away at the living tissue of the caterpillar from the inside, the larvae eventually bore their way out through its skin and the caterpillar dies.

Many caterpillars have protective hairs that can give a very painful sting or cause a long-lasting rash.

Even the pupa of the magpie moth wears warning colours of black and yellow stripes to protect itself from attack.

Many clearwing moths look just like wasps, with transparent wings, wasp-like antennae and a black and yellow-striped body pattern. This helps keep enemies away.

Butterflies and moths are part of the general diet of these predators. However, some wasps specialize in capturing caterpillars, which they **paralyse** with a sting and feed alive to their own larvae. Most adult butterflies and some moths can escape from spider webs because their scales do not stick to the web threads. However, one **nocturnal** spider uses a long ladder-like web, so that before the moth has fallen to the bottom it has lost enough scales to stick to the web.

Many large moth caterpillars are thickly covered in long, stinging spines. These protect them from most enemies and make them very painful to handle. In fact, one caterpillar is so poisonous that its sting can kill a human.

against larger animals, such as birds. Any bird eating these caterpillars would become very ill. However, as most of these caterpillars also taste pretty revolting, the birds usually change their minds after a peck.

POISON PROTECTION

Birds are among the main enemies of butterflies and moths, and a variety of defences are used by the insects in order to avoid being eaten. Many caterpillars feed on poisonous plants and are specially **adapted** to deal with them. They can actually absorb the poisons into their own bodies and use them as chemical protection

Many day-flying moths sport warning colours and are easily mistaken for butterflies. This is the scarlet tiger moth. Tiger moths are found throughout the world and they tend to be brightly coloured.

day-flying moths, such as the scarlet tiger, and the bright orange coloration of the monarch butterfly are good examples of this.

PROTECTION

In order to try and avoid being attacked in the first place, many caterpillars have developed a kind of 'keep off' warning sign, usually made up of brightly coloured patterns that **predators** can easily recognize and remember. These warning colours may be stripes or bands of bold, contrasting colours, such as black and red or black and yellow.

When a caterpillar eventually becomes an adult, the poisons in its body are usually still there. So, not surprisingly, the adult also wears warning colours, although these are often very different from those of the caterpillar. The flashy colours common with many

Because the warning 'uniform' of many adult butterflies and moths is easily recognized by predators, other **species** make use of them as well. In fact, many kinds of bad-tasting but unrelated butterflies and moths all look confusingly similar. This is called a **mimicry** ring.

A few butterflies and moths that are not poisonous also take part in these mimicry rings. Small numbers of perfectly wholesome and tasty butterflies that mimic – or copy – the warning patterns and colours of the bad-tasting bunch can protect themselves from attack. Birds avoid the wholesome 'mimics' on sight, just as if they were the bad-tasting real thing.

Clever camouflage

Good-tasting butterflies and moths generally try to avoid being spotted by their enemies. Many species are camouflaged, allowing them to blend into bark, leaves or flowers. Some look very much like a natural but **inedible** object in their environment. Many caterpillars, and even some **pupae** and adult moths, look like twigs, while others look just like tattered dead leaves.

A wet, shiny bird dropping may seem an unlikely thing to be copied, but several kinds of caterpillars do just that, like those of the swallowtail butterfly family. Many adult moths, such as the Chinese character and a few adult butterflies also look like bird droppings.

MISLEADING APPEARANCES

As well as copying one another's warning patterns, butterflies and moths – both as caterpillars and adults – **mimic** a variety of other creatures in order to try to fool or startle a possible enemy.

Many caterpillars, especially of sphinx moths, have eye-like spots behind the head or on the underside of the body. If suddenly touched, the caterpillar hides its real head and brings these spots into view. What was originally just a harmless caterpillar now appears to be a large-eyed and dangerous-looking snake! Some moths, like the one-eyed sphinx moth, suddenly open their brownish forewings to reveal a pair of huge staring eye spots on their hindwings. Most birds are rather nervous creatures, so when unexpectedly confronted with this large 'face' staring at them, they are sure to take flight.

The 'eyes' of this swallowtail butterfly caterpillar are not real, but fake markings that look like a snake's eyes. The real eyes are very tiny, as in all caterpillars.

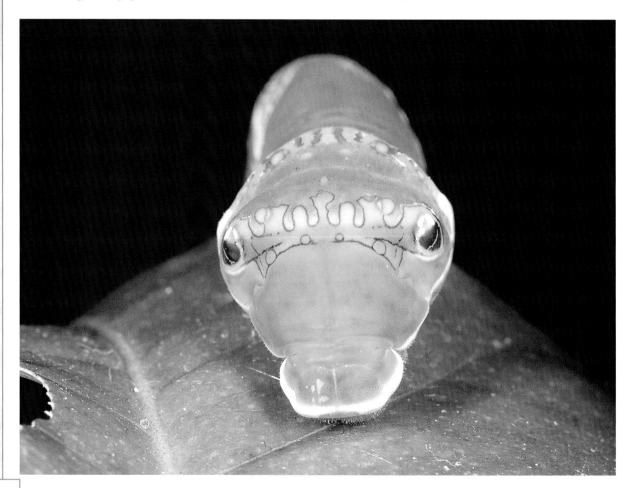

Many clearwing moths, such as this one from South Africa, look amazingly like wasps. Wasps have a nasty sting, so this harmless moth fools many of its enemies into leaving it alone.

FALSE HEADS

Birds will usually try to take their first lethal peck at their prey's head, having been attracted by the eyes. To take advantage of this, some butterflies – particularly in the blue and hairstreak families – have 'false heads' on the tips of their hindwings. These are designed to draw attention away from the real head. If a bird lunges with its beak, it ends up with some scraps of useless wingtip, while the butterfly flutters off in the opposite direction. Some caterpillars also have a false head at the rear end. This is often armoured, so that it can withstand a peck, and is marked with eye-like spots.

Hibernation and migration

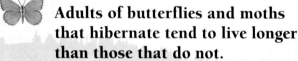
Adults of butterflies and moths that hibernate tend to live longer than those that do not.

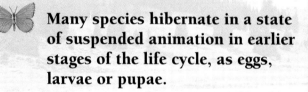
Many species hibernate in a state of suspended animation in earlier stages of the life cycle, as eggs, larvae or pupae.

Most butterflies migrate within 3 metres of the ground, but migrating monarch butterflies have been seen flying across New York, USA at a height of 300 metres.

Butterflies can be picked up by storm fronts and carried many, many kilometres from their migration path thousands of metres high in the air.

HIBERNATION

In cool, temperate lands such as Europe and the USA, many different adult moths and butterflies spend the winter in a sleep-like state known as **hibernation**. They may enter buildings to spend the winter in the shady corner of a room. Caves or hollow trees, or behind thick tangles of ivy, are more natural sleeping places. Some moths and butterflies hibernate together in enormous numbers, and each new generation gathers together in the same place to do so year after year.

MIGRATION

Many moths and butterflies make amazingly long journeys in huge numbers from one place to another, in order to take advantage of fresh vegetation or to avoid overcrowding in their original home. This is known as **migration**, and happens mainly in springtime in temperate countries or after rain in deserts.

The most famous and best-studied migrating butterfly is the

These monarch butterflies are in their winter home of Mexico, where millions of them settle on the trees. By early spring they have all migrated north.

American monarch. With the coming of spring, millions of monarchs wake up from hibernation and move north, laying eggs on their milkweed **foodplants** as they go. They die after laying their eggs. Some of their offspring get as far as Canada during the summer and make the long migration south to Mexico again in the autumn.

Escaping the heat

In hot, dry areas it is the burning summer heat and drought, rather than the cold winter, that create problems for adult butterflies and moths. A few kinds escape the heat by finding a cool spot to spend the summer; this is called **aestivation**. In Australia, brown bogong moths gather in huge numbers among the rocky summits of the Snowy Mountains to aestivate.

41

Butterflies, moths and people

 Some butterflies and moths live in special nature reserves set up just for them.

 Collectors have paid as much as £750 for rare species of butterflies.

 Many monarch butterflies die in their winter homes. Local people gather their wings and use them to make brooches to sell to visitors.

HABITAT DESTRUCTION

Humans have had a very negative effect on most butterflies and moths. The main problem is the destruction of the **habitats** in which they live, especially the **tropical** rainforests that hold the majority of **species**. The spread of towns and cities has also destroyed habitats. The widespread use of **pesticides** has poisoned many species that are normally not harmful to crops. Huge plantations of single crops, such as coffee, tea, potatoes, wheat, rubber and tobacco, now cover the ground where forests or grassland rich in butterflies and moths once stood.

Collection of some of the rarer species has also been a problem. Very high sums of money are paid for certain species. Large-scale collecting for display in wall-mounted cases and for making butterfly jewellery still takes place.

Rainforest clearance and destruction and large-scale farming have been responsible for the decline of many butterflies and moths in recent years. Large numbers of species have become extinct before they have even been given a name.

Moths as helpers and pests

Moths can both harm and help humankind. On the downside, there is the European gypsy moth, which was accidentally released into the wild in North America. It is now a serious pest, destroying huge areas of forest and costing enormous amounts of money to control. On the upside, the silk moth has been kept for more than 2000 years in Asia. The huge **cocoon** spun by the caterpillar gives silk, one of the most prized of all clothing fabrics.

I DIDN'T KNOW THAT

If you want to attract butterflies to your garden, try planting masses of their favourite flowers like daisies and others that are good sources of nectar and attractive to butterflies.

Although many species of butterflies and moths disappeared before we even knew they existed, new species are constantly being found. One Brazilian lepidopterist has discovered no fewer than 4000 new species of moths over the last 20 years.

CONSERVATION

Many butterflies and moths are now protected by the conservation movement. Breeding programmes have been started in such countries as Malaysia, Thailand and New Guinea to ensure a supply of some of the rarer species.

You can do your part towards conserving butterflies and moths by planting a garden containing some of your local native wildflowers. This will provide food for both the caterpillars and adult butterflies.

Glossary

adapt change features of the body or way of life to suit living in a particular place

aestivation hot, dry period some animals spend in a sleep-like state

androconia special scent-scales found on male butterflies

antenna sense organ that sticks out from the adult's head

cocoon silk covering that a caterpillar spins around itself before turning into a pupa

compound eye eye with many tiny lenses common in most adult insects

dormant sleep-like state in which something is alive but not active or growing

echolocation locating the size and range of an object (for example, an insect in flight) by making sounds that reflect off the target and are picked up by the ears

foodplant plant used as food by the larval stage of a butterfly or moth

habitat natural home of an animal or plant

hibernation state of deep sleep in which some animals pass the cold months of winter

identify recognize or know what something is

inedible not fit to be eaten

light trap box containing a light which moths (attracted by the light) find easy to get into and hard to get out of

metamorphosis change that takes place within the pupa to produce an adult insect

migration seasonal movement of animals from one location to another

mimic animal that copies another one through similar behaviour, coloration, etc.

nocturnal animal or insect that is active at night

nutrient (nutritious) substance which feeds or nourishes a plant or animal, and helps it to grow

ocelli tiny, simple eyes not able to make out an image

paralyse cause something to be unable to move

parasite animalvery hot and humidther, but does not kill it; many parasites of butterflies and moths should really be called parasitoids, because they eventually kill their 'host', usually a caterpillar

pesticide chemical used to kill insects and other pests on crops

predator animal that hunts other animals for food

pupation resting stage following the larval stage (or caterpillar) during which transformation to the adult insect takes place

skipper kind of small butterfly, often brown, that has characteristics of both moths and butterflies

sodium soft, white metal found in salt

solar energy energy that comes from the Sun's rays

species kind or type of animal

style part of the female organs of a flower

territory area defended by males, to which females are likely to come for mating

tropical very hot and humid

Further information

Books

Britain's Butterflies, David Tomlinson (WildGuides, 2002)

Collins Wild Guide: Butterflies and Moths of Britain and Europe, John Still (Collins, 1996)

The Illustrated Encyclopedia of Butterflies, John Feltwell (Grange Books, 2001)

The Pocket Guide to the Butterflies of Britain and Europe, Paul Whalley and Richard Lewington (Mitchell Beazley, 2000)

The Wildlife Trusts Guide to Butterflies and Moths, Nicholas Hammond (series editor) (New Holland Publishers, 2002)

Websites

www.enchantedlearning.com/subjects/butterfly

www.butterfly-conservation.org

Disclaimer
All the Internet addresses (URLs) given in this book were valid at the time of going to press. However, due to the dynamic nature of the Internet, some addresses may have changed, or sites may have ceased to exist since publication. While the author and publishers regret any inconvenience this may cause readers, no responsibility for any such changes can be accepted by either the author or the publishers.

Index

Numbers in *italic* indicate pictures

abdomen 7
aestivation 41, *41*
African moon moth 21, *21*
Agrippa moth 6
American Great Basin fritillary butterfly 16
American tent-caterpillar moth 25
androconia 22
antennae 7, 8, 12, *12*, 13, 21, *21*, 25, 27
ants, partnership with 25, *25*
apple codling moth 15
Asian vampire moth 33

bagworm moth 10
bell moth 15
black swallowtail butterfly 20
blue butterfly family 15, 19, 31, 39
bogong moth 41, *41*
brimstone butterfly 12, *12*
brown butterfly 15
brush-footed butterfly family 15, 23, *23*

California tent moth 31
camouflage 28, 37, *37*
carpenterworm moth 30
caterpillars 6, 14, 15, 18
    bodies and growth 24, 26, *26*, 27, 28,
    28, 29, 30
    enemies and self-defence 34, 35, *35*,
    36, 37, *37*, 38, *38*, 39
    (*see also food and feeding*)
Chinese character moth 37
chrysalis (see pupa, pupae)
cinnabar moth caterpillar 27, *27*
claspers 26, *27*
clearwing butterfly 10, *10*, 16
clearwing moth 34, 39, *39*
clothes moth 15
cocoon 24, 28, *28*, 29, 43
collectors 42

colours 12, 13, *13*, 14-15
    warning 34, 36, *36*, 39, *39*
comma butterfly 29, *29*
conservation 43
copper butterfly 15, 25
courtship 20-22, *20*

death's head hawkmoth 30
defence tactics 34-39, *34*, *35*, *36*, *37*, *38*, *39*
desert habitat 16, 18-19, *18*

'ears' 7
echolocation 7
eggs 24-25, *24*, 26, *26*
elephant hawkmoth 15, *15*
emperor moth 15, 24, *24*
European gypsy moth 43
eye spots on wings 15, 38
eyes (adult) 7, 8
    (caterpillar) 26, 27

'false heads' 39
families of butterflies and moths 14
feelers (see antennae)
flannel moth 24
flying 10-11, 14, *15*
food and feeding (adult) 9, *9*, *14*, 16, 32-33,
    32, *33*
    (caterpillar) 25, *25*, 26, *26*, 27, *27*, 30-31,
    30, *31*
frangipani hawkmoth 30, *30*
fritillary butterfly *14*, 15, 16, 19

giant skipper 18
glasswing butterfly 10, 17
grassland habitat 16, 19
great purple hairstreak butterfly 20

habitat destruction 42-43, *42*
habitats 16-19
hair pencils 22
hairstreak butterfly 19, 39

harvester butterfly 33
hawkmoth (see also sphinx moth) 9, *9*, 10, 15
heath fritillary butterfly 14, *14*
hibernation 40
hummingbird hawkmoth 9, *9*

identification of butterflies and moths 12-15

large white butterfly 8, *8*, 24, 31, *31*
larva, larvae (see caterpillars)
leaf mine 31, *31*
leopard moth 30
lepidoptera 6
lepidopterist 6, 43
life cycle 24-29
lifespan 24
longhorn moth 20-21, *20*
long-tailed skipper 14, *14*

magpie moth 34
malachite longwing butterfly 17, *17*
mandible 26
mating 20-23, *20*, *22*, *23*
maxilla 26
metamorphosis 28-29, *28*, *29*
migration 40-41, *40-41*
mimicry 36-38
moult 27, *27*, 28
monarch butterfly 10, 15, 20, 27, *27*, 28, *28*,
    32, 36, 40-41, *40-41*
moon moth 11, 21, *21*
mourning cloak butterfly 15

ocelli 26, 27
one-eyed sphinx moth 38
owl butterfly 26, *26*

painted lady butterfly 19, *19*
palp 26
parasites 34
poisons used in defence 35, 36
predators 34-35
    protection against 25, 29, 34-39, *35*, *36*,
    37, *38*, *39*

proboscis 7, 9, 32
prolegs 26, 27
pupa, pupae 18, 24, 28-29, *28*, *29*, *29*
pygmy blue butterfly 6

Queen Alexandra's birdwing butterfly 6

rainforest habitat 16-17, *16-17*, 42, *42*

scarlet tiger moth 36, *36*
scent 8, 20, 21, 22
silk 26, 43
silk moth 26, 43
skipper 14, *14*, 18, 19
smell, sense of 7, 8, 20, 21, *21*, 22
speckled wood butterfly 20
sphinx moth (see also hawkmoth) 9, 15, 38
spinneret 26
spiracles 26
spurge hawkmoth 12, *12*
sulphur butterfly family (see whites)
swallowtail butterfly 7, *7*, 11, *11*, 14, 17, 37,
    37, 38, *38*

tail 11, 14
taste, sense of 25
temperate forest habitat 19
thorax 7
transparent-winged butterflies 10, *10*
true legs 26, 27

white admiral butterfly 25
whites butterfly family 14-15
wings 6, 7, 10-11, *10*, *11*, 12-13, *12*, *13*
wing scales 6, 10, 13, *13*, 34, 35
winter moth 10

yucca moth 18, *18*